SAXONS IN THE GARDEN

Barbara Jordi

SAXONS IN THE GARDEN
Poems of the Saxon Shore Way

Barbara Dordi

Illustrations by Russi Dordi

SAWD
BOOKS

For Ann and Bacha

ACKNOWLEDGEMENTS

Some of these poems have appeared in the following publications:
Partnership (Community of Poets Press, 1994, *Transition* (Community of Poets Press, 1995) *Trust* (Community of Poets Press, 1995, *The Poets's Palette* (Poetry Now, 1995), *Kent Poetry Anthology* (The Aegis Press, 1995).

The cover design is by Russi Dordi.

SAWD
BOOKS

Plackett's Hole, Bicknor
Sittingbourne, Kent ME9 8BA

SAWD BOOKS is an imprint of SAWD Publications

A CIP catalogue record for this book is available from
The British Library
ISBN: 1 872489 15 X
Copyright 1995 by Barbara Dordi

ILLUSTRATIONS

Map

CONTENTS

Introduction

INTRODUCTION

This book has come into being as a result of walking 140 miles of the Kent coastline from Gravesend to Rye as it allegedly was in Saxon times.

The main source of information concerning the walk itself came from Saxon Shore Way guides produced on behalf of the Kent Area of the Ramblers Association in co-operation with the Footpaths Section of the Kent County Council. They have divided the route into ten sections, from six to twenty miles in length. Each section has been divided up into shorter stretches to enable a return to be made to the starting point using public transport. The instructions and sketch maps are very clear, but we bought OS Pathfinder Maps for each region as a backup as well as for extra information and interest.

My husband Russi and I usually take fifteen minutes to walk a mile, but on the Shore Way walk, we averaged thirty minutes. The difference allows for taking photographs, consulting maps, guides, and trying to find disappearing paths or elusive stiles. In the end, we found that the walk had divided itself up into twenty three sections, our average walk being about six miles.

During the eighteen months we took to walk the Shore Way, we travelled over a thousand miles by car to and from the start of each section. We rarely did a circular walk, always opting to get back by either bus, train, or car (if we were fortunate enough to have friends with us). The only round trip we did was by bicycle from our home town Herne Bay, to Whitstable

It has been a fascinating project - showing us parts of the county we would never have visited otherwise, and making us see the Kent we were familiar with in a very different light. We have marvelled at the beauty and richness of the county's flora and fauna, and have been inspired to delve into its extraordinary history.

We have met interesting people from all walks of life who have been generous with anecdotes and memories of their unique experiences of living and working here

We have enjoyed walking and working together: each privately being moved by the same experience in different ways, painting sparking off poetry and vice versa, or both going in completely independent directions. Walking the Saxon Shore Way has given us a curious sense of identity with the path as well as a particular familiarity with, and affection for Kent. I can thoroughly recommend getting out there and experiencing it for yourself.

Barbara Dordi

SAXONS IN THE GARDEN
(For Rachel)

Saxons in 'The Garden'
please show yourselves today,
all the Kentish children
would like to come and play.

Tell them all the place names
you left us with in Kent,
like cliff, combe, ham and weald,
and also what they meant.

Tell them where you came from
in 449 BC.
Show them on the map where
you sailed across the sea.

Tell them of your homeland -
show them how you dressed,
tell them of your armour,
I'm sure they'll like that best.

Show them all your path ways
around the Kentish shore,
marked by special sign stones -
horned helmets by the score:

Stone ones, wooden, concrete too,
iron, plastic (just a few),
tall ones, short ones, fat, thin, strong,
grey ones, red ones, round, square, long.

A hundred and forty miles,
not one of them a bore,
a living history book,
the county's Saxon Shore.

QUICK STILL

This bulwark shore
holds forever
strong Saxons,
her mud fast
on firm limbs.
Our forbears sleep,
rude cloth ironed,
creased by layers -
converging force
of successive
generations.

Ham, ton, bridge, burgh,
stead, ford, hurst, mere:
they are still here.

Would they sharpen their swords
for the Kent of today?
Ships redundant,
they'd come charging through The Tunnel,
then stop. Amazed.....
Vampire Progress
guzzled history,
suckling its seed
on the soft sleeping land.

They'd make the headlines though -
SAXONS BEATEN BY RAPE & PILLAGE CO.

PALE FACE

Weak winter sun squanders itself -
concrete, chimneys, derricks, iron.

Deserted streets whisper their plight
in echoes of hollow footsteps.

Pocohontas, frozen in flight,
stares forever seaward.

Fast Tilbury ferry froths at the mouth -
only four passengers.

Gulls flap in and out of their squat -
the once-elegant Town pier.

Sunday roasts from riverside flats
steal upstream to the capital.

The Thames retreats; bottles and crates
cans and anchor flukes spike the mud.

Asian families on the promenade -
greens, oranges, vibrant purples;
hybrid orchids brave the cold,
make pale Gravesend a Gauguin.

KHARTOUM TIME

Under polystyrene,
under seaweed and shells
of the Thames' high water mark
they lie:
Saxons, invisible,
until we walk their Shore Way.

Above grey stone rubble,
above brambles and weeds
of General Gordon's fort,
bare sky:
Shornmead, demolished,
until we think of Khartoum.

In gun emplacements
with misty river views we rest,
in a time warp we take shelter:
soldiers, scarlet-clad,
leap into the day,
firing technicolour.

MONSTERS

Pterodactyl head surfaces
just beyond Gravesend:
fossilised Isle
parting the sea
between mighty Thames
and lesser Medway.

Astride eye-socket hills
once orchard clad,
steel-grey power stations
clamp the skull fast,
darken bare-ribbed fields
stripped clean of trees,
snorting smoke to Europe
..................*silently.*

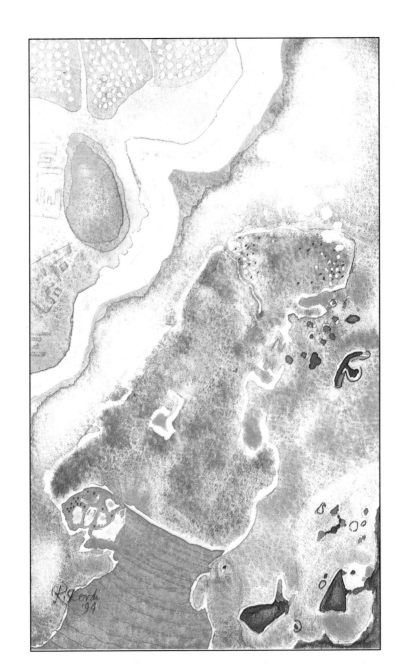

BIRD'S EYE VIEW

That day a single gull was gliding
the gloom that refused to blue itself -
brooding over blood turned rust.

It had just scanned sewage farm, rubbish tip,
taking its pick, hooked bill expert
dealing with the wreckage we create.

It soared over naked brown fields -
protruding flint bones skimming back
glinting arrows from sky's shafts.

A speck of dust in a beam of light,
it skirted Kingnorth's chimney,
solitary pointer on the horizon.

It floated towards the Thames, webbed feet ready
to tread water that reflected the day:
sultry, only flashes of red in the grey.

DAY LIGHTS

Fading flowers
Scattered showers
Seeded power
Virgin's Bower.

Glowing sunshine
Bright red berry
Decorations
Hip haw merry.

Filtering sun
Transfigured whites
Filaments gleam
Christmas day lights.

STROOD, SUNDAY

- so serene,
Cliffs of chalk topped with green,
Ancient church reaching high,
Winter sun, clear blue sky.
Seagulls scream gliding low,
River boats to and fro,
Spindly trees shake their hair,
People stroll, take the air.

Strood Monday
- pouring rain,
Chalk cliffs grey, on the wane,
Frindsbury church seen no more,
Clouds of smoke screen the shore,
Breakers yards bang and hiss,
Lorries roar, swerve to miss
Buses, bikes, cars galore,
'DON'T WALK' five days more.

WATCHING

Men kill in the name of peace:
battlements of pock-marked stone -
Rochester Keep, highest in the land.

Men kill in the name of faith:
leaden spires impale the sky -
cathedral for God invisible.

Built almost side by side,
by men of peace for men of war
and God of love,
each keeps a wary eye
on the other.

THE MEDWAY WAS CONTENT

- it's water sweet as mead,   it

Flowed gently on through Roman
and Saxon invasions;   it

Saw Queen Bess build stone castles
along its wooded banks;   it

Didn't turn a hair when the Dutch
advanced on Chatham;   it

Even helped bargemen turn
tan-sailed boats laden with coal;   its

Tides brought in fresh fish,
always guaranteed clean water,   then

Medway was conscripted.

Diverted,   it forgot its natural way
                                          to the sea,

then   lost, it forged new routes,
                                   searching detritus of ages;

then   dirty, it spewed out rubbish
                                   to swallow it next tide;

then   came plastic - buckets, bags, nets;
                                        polystyrene, cartons;

then   will the sunken explosives ship
                                   redeem its sweet name?

LOWER HALSTOW CHURCH

Nestled in marsh land
fed by winding creeks
brimming with birds,
St. Margaret of Antioch,
simple Saxon church,
unsung jewel set on a mound,
a beacon for all at sea.
Of flint and Kentish ragstone
and herring-boned Roman tiles -
a living ministry still,
in this ancient holy place.

Folk always tilled soil here,
made homes from clay beneath,
harvested a rich sea.   Now,
brickworks razed, sea polluted -
hulks litter forsaken creeks,
red-raw houses line the shore.
And medieval wall paintings
once hidden beneath whitewash?
Carved Jacobean pulpit?
The aged lead font?
Church cherished her treasures.

TURNER MAGIC

- and slagheaps
become spectacular mountains
silhouetted in the fire
of evening sky - a sky painted with steam:
tints of yellow, orange, red
and pale, pale purple.

Intricate reed bed foreground
weaves in the daytime picture
with teal and whimbrel - stilled now:
firm textured tonality.

Chimneys, the paper-mill, charcoaled
squarely on the horizon - made benign;
smoke snakes chameleon sky:
kinetic evening sculpture.

Quick, look,
hold your breath;
fix it firmly
in the gallery of your mind.

FAT BOTTOM GIRLS

Bessie, Beryl and Beatrice Maud,
Edith, Esther, Emily Lloyd:
fat bottom girls - tar-black and long,
great beamy girls - forty tons strong;
these barges once a well-known sight
on East Coast shores, morning to night.

When fully canvassed - white or tan,
they sailed the swatchways - like Saltpan;
you'd hear them chuckle as water passed
seductive sterns - these girls were fast.
To Thames from Medway or the Swale,
they ferried straw by the bale,

Or bricks, cement, and even sand
loaded from gutways near to land.
For shoal waters they were made
but skipper and mate often strayed
from winding creeks to crested seas -
sleek modern girls have nothing on these.

ELEGY FOR A BARGE

Ousted by the lorry,
they just dumped you here
ignominiously.

If you had been a horse
you would have been put out
to far kinder pasture.

Torn ribs belly skyward
to a deck long since picked clean
by greedy decades;

Her skeleton wafts to
and fro to the tune
of brackish water's making.

I must play Charon,
steer her final passage,
toll already paid:

Time's garment is unpicked,
a hundred years of wool
gathered in,

Vera, resplendent,
tan sails filled,
glides silently into the sea's embrace

SLEEP, BEAUTY

Before the spell you wound inland
carried barges to the wooden jetty
and waiting gangers glad of work.
They loaded bricks, hay or cement -
horsedrawn carts wheeled through your mud.

Ambling ways kept you safe
from wind's heavy knife sculpting
pointed waves, in cahoots with the
scouring tide of the Swale without:
your isolation preserved you.

Spell cast, you left no documents
to furnish sea-dog tales; just
the jetty, ghostly silhouette now,
creek silt-sinking under Progress
and five decades before the kiss.

GEOLOGY LESSON

Don't believe the cartography.
From Rainham to Faversham
one whole strata's gone missing.

They carved up rich topsoil,
plundered the virgin clay,
then flung the soil back again -

For millions of cheap, Kent bricks
barged to London for schools,
industry, The Underground.

Walk these sunken fields today
where blinded brickworks line up
with the thousands unemployed.

Witness the fate of the hard
won yellow brick: substantial
factories and schools silenced,

Bulldozed, buried - the hard-core
of designed obsolescence.
Don't believe the cartography.

RUBBISH TIP HILLS

Vibrant green hill
Perfectly even mound
Planted with trees
In plastic protectors,
Like W.W.1.tombstones
Row upon even row
Stiff with new life.

Half an egg hill -
A chocolate Easter egg.
Not sweet-filled -
Not disappointingly
Hollow too,
Just stuffed with the rubbish
Rats once rummaged through:

Sindy dolls limbs askew
Clutching ash, burned right through,
Dirt-filled cups, chipped, green,
These detergents can't get clean,
 Rags torn to shreds by mice,
 Foam pillows home to lice,
 So much more out of sight.
 "Well then, that's all right!"

Soon, they'll be in
Biesty's Incredible Cross-sections book.
I hope I'm not around
When these instant hills
Cave-in
And shrivel,
Like limp balloons.

OARE MARSHES NATURE RESERVE

Take your seats -
the concert is free
if you sit very still.

From this wilderness of tussocks
a snipe's cry reverberates.
Kingfisher - in a blue flash - gone.
His high piping lingering ......

Curlews chorus in trembling song,
smaller redshank swelling the sound
with down-slurred calls; and a heron
watches, listening. Then flaps.

Here in 1916,
the Explosive Works Ensemble
(heard as far away as Norfolk)
played a different tune:

One blue spark, saffron smoke....
UP went the buildings, one, two, three,
UP went the workers, cheap rag dolls;
smoke erased sun, river protested.

Over a hundred killed -
a sell out.

KENT HOPS

CLOCKWISE
- through centuries they climb
high poles, wires geometric,
corkscrewing skyward, sunning
green wasps nests of petals - cache
of special flavouring for beer;
Kent hops fermented Jack Cade's rebellion,
fired hopes of farmers each September,
and hoards of pickers from London town,
quenching real ale patrons,
claiming the lager crown.

WINTER LANDSCAPE
In Hilder's dry-brush stubble fields
bare fan trees lace pale horizons,
one o'clock nests caught at midday,
rooks suspend in wet on wet skies;
his bulging matrons - warm brick oasts,
perfect roundels for drying hops,
upturned cornets their red tile roofs,
tipped white with candle-snuffer cowls:
Kent's crumbling emblem conserved.
What art to keep the hop encircling?

FAVERSHAM BREW
This yeasty smell means all is well
wafting medley of buildings
soaring pitched roofs, finials,
columned guildhall's cupola,
seeping through dormers of every age,
tree-lined Abbey Street and Market Place;

Not from plump hops set in pillars,
glossy pargeting ever green
entwining the Faversham scene,
but from vital hops the brewery grows,
in spite of the French and British trade.
Long may the town's essence pervade.

HERE

You felt it, that's why you're here
walking the narrow creekside path
being caressed by blossom;
it bobs, sways, reaches out -
luminous, in soft English light.

You surge with the highest tide
when creek pretends he's river;
and on the embankment, sedges,
brown busby heads on slender stalks,
nod in elastic salute.

Grass bounds back, you leave no track;
reedbeds line your way - fine strokes
of pink and ochre reaching tall.
And that far creamy mass?
A profusion of lacy umbels.

Above your head the May bends boughs
which sway to frenzied feeding birds;
no other sound here at all -
but the hoarse cuckoo call -
and you, your blood racing.

WHITSTABLE TO HERNE BAY
BY BICYCLE

We flew along the seawall -
very very quickly,
early Sunday morning -
early in June.

We had to stop for colour -
very very often,
glowing in the shingle,
scoured and hard.

Tissue paper petalled -
the yellow-horned poppies,
springing from the grey-green
velvet of leaves.

Have you seen a house like this
adorned with painted frieze -
barges, their tan sails filled
crossing rough seas?

Low tide and Whitstable Street
points a shingle finger -
shall we ride the tightrope,
deep sea both sides?

We pedalled past tidal ponds -
very very quickly,
people dump rubbish here -
carpets, the lot.

We had to stop for skylarks -
.....................just once.

HERNE BAY WINTER

Cold mist plasters his hair; he smiles.
Beach silent, promenade bare; it is his.
His dog stalks, barks a daily excitement.
Towers loom in and out through mist:
far Reculver, once Roman fort,
now sad, caravan clad.
Ragged waves rush wooden groynes to spume. Pause.
Then slink back gurgling, seething.

Out to sea, gentler waves daub
cybernetic brown on grey. He stares,
intent on the broken pier. He mends it -
he's a boy again: family, friends, sun,
home-made swim suits heavy with salt; laughing,
they race over pebbles into a warm sea....
The panting dog intrudes.
"Let's go boy." He knows the way.

The peace of a Herne Bay winter
when the 'Improvements' are done?
New harbour, imported sand,
(Not a word about the band-stand),
Victorian lampposts (brand new),
paying car-parks, swimming pool too.
They'll all come flocking, money to spend.
Will he be the one to pay..........at the end?

GIVING BACK

He floats a thin, pale wash
across the sky. Before it's dry
he works in tones to make it bleed
into a dull day on Wantsum marsh.
Two dabs with his One Stroke brush -
Reculver's skeleton Towers.
Just for fun he turns monochrome marsh
into waving meadow.
He stipples in a rash of villages:
Lilliput by giant blots -
Richborough power station.
A deft stroke with a Number 6
and Thanet Way snakes grey.

His Magic Eye
locks on landscape,
mesmerized;
centuries flash by
in seconds:

The sea retreats -
stone and red tiles rise from ruins,
sweep landward, erase the Towers -
Regulbium fort reborn.
Sandbanks are scoured,
seawalls smash,
marshes are swallowed whole -
the Wantsum bursts into being.
Phoenix-like, Retupiae returns
to champion the eastern sky.
Below forested hills
hamlets line fertile plains
fed by a brimming Wantsum.

His brushes conjure
white autumn mists;
marshes vanish
east to west
and that wide, ghostly channel returns.

CONVERSATION PIECE

Castle to Power Station, Richborough
Even from my ruins I look down
on you and your smooth operations:
that chimney and those towers....
Macbeth and the witches.

When I was a lad, the Wantsum flowed
where you stand now, feet in clay.
Think you're grand? You've no idea son.
They'll dynamite you one day

You reply with a puff. A sinister spell?
You're cursed too and you do spoil the view.
Never think you'll ever get
'Listed Building' slapped on you.

My people knew how to build -
a Roman arch stood inside my walls.
I commanded, enhanced the view.
You won't last. Don't fit in. I do.

Reply
I have to look up - you on the hill,
visible on clear days only:
stone and mortar - a mottled line of wall -
crumbling fast, leaning, soon to fall.

From the moment of inception, I rose,
female curves embracing sky,
rivalling nature I've heard sculptors say;
I may make the Turner Prize some day....

Cousin Battersea - great cream smoke stacks -
pure Expressionism architects saved.
How can you think you improve the view -
soon there'll be nothing left of you?

My smooth concrete improves with age.
My presence benefits everyone around.
You're deluded, you've had your day.
Make way for progress. I'm here to stay

GO

Brush your way through tall wheat,
ochre ripe and prickly stiff;
suck milk from its ears,
bite hard on summer's grain,
stubborn husks caught in your teeth.

Launch clouds of seedheads in your way -
the dandelion nearly done;
drink the pink, white, perfect
stripes of bindweed,
Warrior Queen of the field.

Before ploughs comb the earth in rows -
stripping her of all she grows.
Before straggler leaves are strewn on paths
by trees loath to give up their last.
Before mist makes midday miss its cue.

WHERE ENGLAND BEGAN

Under the knuckle of Thanet,
gulls scream impatience for the ebb,
dream fat-pickings on mud flats
five centuries in the making
by a sea that sucked Wantsum,
and spewed this gaping bay:
Ramsgate, haughty in the distance,
Sandwich, now trapped a mile inland,
once took ships' warps ashore.

Boats felt the pull of this land,
forced by strong-armed beacons
Dover, Ramsgate, ever white
into Stour's waiting arms,
to be pushed to Canterbury,
in the wake of Augustine.

Hengist and Horsa felt it,
landed vast longships:
Saxons crunched, scraped ashore,
the prancing white horse
taming fierce Roman eagles;
Britain invaded once more.

See the past excavated into life
by the pounding of our mentor, sea;
here, where England began.

LORD WARDEN OF THE CINQUE PORTS - HIS COMFORTER

He'd just come out to India.
We were in lines on parade, he inspecting.
When he reached me, he paused, almost passed on,
then leaned back, casual like,
tapped me on the chest with his gloves,
said to the commanding officer, " He'll do".

I went knocking at his door.
(This was going to be my big break).
"You will be responsible for my campaign bed".
What an honour!

The bed was very special.
A brass frame,
leather webbing,
a canvas base,
horsehair mattress.
And that's just the bed.
The bolster was made of horsehair
covered in leather;
the quilt and mattress covers -
blue silk.

For eight years I lugged that bed
from one battle to the next.
In all that heat.
It was damned hard work, I can tell you!
All he had to do was to plan campaigns.

I began to hope the bed would be stolen, broken,
the mattress infested even.
Bloody thing was as impervious as its master.
Was I glad when the Mahratta chiefs
had been defeated.
Now I could go home to a decent climate.
A different posting. Ah.

*   *   *

After a couple of years back in Blighty
I was summoned to Spain.
(My talents hadn't gone unnoticed then).

When I got there, he was waiting with -
yes.......... you've guessed it -
that bleeding campaign bed.
Well, this time it was for just four years
Four long, heavy years.
I was pig sick .
I mean - what a job!

I tried all kinds of subterfuge
to lose that bed.
Nothing worked!

I tried diplomatic tactics:
a lighter, more portable modern bed
was surely more fitting
for such an important officer
serving King and Country abroad?

No. He'd "grown attached to it".
Said he just couldn't plan campaigns
if it wasn't in his room.
Sort of talisman, he said it had become.

The bed was beginning to get a sort of fame -
well, he was, for sleeping on such a tough,
and by now, old thing.
But as I said to my mates, I said -
it's no harder than the ground we have to sleep on -
and it's a darned sight drier!
Drier....
It was then that I resorted to meanness.
Well, a chap can take only so much.

First I used it as a piss pot -
hoping to rot the horse hair,
the silk cover,

the leather webbing,
tarnish the brass too, perhaps.

Would you believe it?
He didn't even notice!

I soon stopped that.

After all - he was only sleeping on it.
I was the one who had to
put it up,
take it down,
cart it around,
guard it with my life, etc. etc.

Was I glad when we'd sent the French scarpering.
Now I could go home.
Get a decent posting.

*   *   *

Only this time, he wouldn't let me go.
Said he might need me sooner rather than later.
Great!

*   *   *

Belgium was next.
Well, at least the climate was cooler.
Didn't stop the bed from ponging though.
Or from getting heavier.
Or was it me?
Takes its toll, you know,
carting a great burden like this
from one country to another for -
how many years was it now?
Fourteen, fifteen?
Felt more like fifty!

When we got to Belgium,

things were sort of disorganized
After a few chaotic weeks
I thought of dumping the bed in the Prussian lines -
they were nearest the Frogs.
It was bound to get trampled on there.
Who knows, Boneyface himself might claim it?
Then his man could drag it around for years on end.
Poor bugger!

But before I could do anything,
old clever clogs hit on a plan to beat the Frenchies.
Well, he would wouldn't he?
Anyone who can sleep on a bed in that condition
can put his mind to anything.

We found ourselves in the thick of it again -
cannon to the left,
cannon to the right,
and me in the middle of it all
stuck like glue to this 'ere bed.

It was after this battle
that he became famous,
And I mean famous.
People lined the streets
to welcome him home.......
victorious.

I was with him on that day too.
Minus the bed.
I felt a bit sad at that.
After all,
if it hadn't been for that bed,
and me, of course,
the Iron Duke
could have met his Waterloo
well before 1815.

SHYPPE SWALLOWER

Stripped of island status by angry sea
four miles off shore (eleventh century)
he got the hump, simply couldn't settle...

Just what could he turn his hand to now -
chalk 70 feet under shifting sand?
That's when he thought he'd try his hand -

Galleons first - White Swan, Jonas, Abraham,
rather big for starters, but he managed it -
sip-sucking them in, bit by bit.

Luggers from Deal he found more sticky
but down them he did in full sight of home
and because he'd been drowned - wouldn't atone.

His daily mutations brought such wide acclaim,
that big-wigs in London had heard of his name.
Boats were rigged with fore and aft sails,

To steer better courses - wind up their tails.
But sloop, ketch or cutter - Hope, Mary, Sadak
went the way of the rest on scratching his back.

Steamers like Ashley, Mahratta, Batjan,
were more of a challenge for, by now, the old man.
What fun retching rubber, jute and loose tea

(From far away India) into Dover's cold sea.
This stunt brought in trippers to Deal Pier in droves
They oo'd and they ahhh'd at the great low tide shows.

By now his shipwrecks had filled scores of ledgers
They tried once more to destroy him with dredgers -

He ate *them*. Boats, tackle - even the men.
Boy was he booed when he quaffed our warships.
But cheers went up in all British pubs
when he got indigestion from fat German subs.

In the appalling storm of '54
he thought sea was granting him status once more;
when *that* didn't happen he became so mad -

He swallowed South Goodwin, six men and a lad.
Now all his three lightships will stay unmanned,
in case old Goodwin has more binges planned.

HIGH

Blown here in a gale,
it clings to barbed wire,
grey-white and ragged:
sheep's wool? No,
bubble-wrap.

One of wind's jokes.

Like a cat marking territory
he scours these cliff tops,
flattens flint field crops;
carves topiary art
from trees cringing
to escape his blast.

His always - the last laugh.

FOUND ON DOVER CLIFFS

No dust for you
when your hour came -
fragile shell
petrified in chalk.

The pinpricked star
where spines once rose
to spear survival -
a redundant epitaph.

What a perfect fit
in the palm of my hand.

Foolish, to be alarmed
as I read your print -
alive in death
after 80 million years.

BLUEBIRDS

Heads bowed to escape wind, we fight
our way along cliff tops
perilously near the edge,
in White Cliffs Country -
just Andrew and I.

Passing the new
Battle of Britain Memorial
a Chipmunk from Manston drones overhead.
The Germans! Quick, take cover!
It's W.W.2 again!

It'll be alright
just you wait and see,
Vera Lynn tells us.
And she should know -
she's been through it all before.

Spread-eagled, eyes level with cliff edge
and winging birds feeding on the updraught,
Andrew sees bluebirds
like Disney, toffee, that song.
I know they are not blue enough.

We watch the swallows preparing to leave,
talk about the fact,
the real miracle: their coming back.

Swallows circle above us,
petalling the air
russet, white and blue.

GOING FOREIGN

Was it really twenty years ago?
We drooled on Dover cliffs,
spotting the odd ferry,
picturing ourselves on it,
France tantalisingly close,
sometimes clear, often not,
but always there, waiting.

At last we've saved the fare!
The ship's engines vibrate
a giant quake, its deafening horn
resonating through to bone.
We're moving, Paul shouts.
Good-bye England, Kathy cries,
will we see you again?

Passengers swarm the stern,
watch white cliffs sucked
under jubilant wake,
gulls screaming the excitement
adults are dumb to utter
until mid Straights,
when they practise their parlez-vous.

A streak on the horizon:
It's cloud.

It's France
What - no cliffs?
Who cares? We're abroad!

*   *   *

Duty relaxed in '94,
France saw bootleggers by the score,
in cars, lorries, the Transit van -
filled to the gunnels till headlines ran,
BRITS DRINK CALAIS DRY.
Dodgem ferries zoom in and out
with seasoned punters now:
day-trippers, granny entrepreneurs,
beer-bellied trolley pushers.
Some don't even disembark.

Duty Frees - blow your brass,
but on which tempting offer?
Open your 200 pack,
smoke like crazy,
never look back;

France, out-of-town superstore.
Not so foreign any more.

ROSEMARY

-lines the forgotten road
where gun batteries ploughed the Leas
and new military were billeted;
steel girders, barbed wire, tinselled
the mined beach for Hitler;
Victoria Pier was breached, then blazed -
funeral pyre of a passing age.

Before this road, imperious hotels
'magnificent sea views from every window'
looked down the length of the tree-lined Leas;
reefers, sailor-suits, boaters, boys with bats,
shawls, long dresses, parasols, large hats -
the English Riviera on parade.

For just one penny go down the cliffs
on modern water and gravity lifts;
snooty travellers don't spare us a glance
on the once-a-day steamer bound for France.
Clank through the pier - iron turnstile,
WHAT THE BUTLER SAW - suppress a smile
'til it's time to waltz - the tea-dance at three,
then back to our lodgings - Milly and me.

SeaCat foams, bubbling with trippers
speeding to France in under an hour,
fleeing fairground and Folkestone Market -
bag-laden shoppers fighting through crowds.
From the curlicued bandstand, music still winds
down zig-zag paths, through tamarisk, and pines;
here's rosemary for yesterday's songs.

BORER

- For Sale. One careful owner -
The Arabs didn't made a bid - exclusive
though it is, like Harrods. One donor

needed for this great white mole, tailor-made
for the engineering feat of the century,
which as yet, hasn't seen much trade.

The Tunnel Exhibition Centre came first,
concrete, steel, tracks, cable - tours twice an hour -
a major tourist attraction from a hearse.

The French now come on le Shuttle, very much overdue,
to arrive at a London station announcing
their hero's defeat - Waterloo.

Some people here vow they'll never go through -
listing the risks: fire, terrorists,
they're concerned about rabies too.

Why fear the Tunnel, when our isolation has gone?
After 7,000 years of waiting,
we can walk where our fathers came from.

BIG GAME

Weather too blustery for umbrellas
left land sodden; then sly sun surprised all,
had us walking by the Military Canal,
just five days before Christmas.

Landward, Lympne Castle, grown high
on ruins of Stutfall tumbling the slope -
a thriving stronghold once, when Rother
sneaked out to sea at Hythe.

Tell-tale tide marks betray the lineage
of sudden grassy rises - cliffs
sea stopped licking centuries ago,
leaving slough to be inned by Romans -

genesis of Romney, the marshes:
triangular apron slung on the county's edge,
criss-cross machined with drainage ditch seams,
Martello Tower bordered.

Tired canal steps the ancient coastline
in measured paces to Winchelsea,
ready for Napoleon who didn't dare,
a facelift its reward - blue signs everywhere.

Quiet verges flank its tree-lined banks,
coaxing Barbour wellies to stroll out with dogs -
deigning to nod as we pass, tutting fiercely
when lions let rip from the zoo park close by.

Three muddy miles more, in fading red light,
a silly flock, herded by the mistake

of our squelching approach, to Aldington Knoll.
Sheep pose; silhouetted in silence:
grey ruffs framing fifteen heads,
primitive masks, pointed, white,

at each apex a black wet blotch,
sucking in the last blood drops of light;

when we move, it moves,
giant head,
multi-cat's-eyes
forcing us through iron gates, pressing us home,

haunting our Christmas,
together, alone.

HYTHE, KENT

After a drawing by Turner (engraved by George Cooke 1824)

This was the moment,
I raised my hand -
and was frozen forever
in an act of command.

Ever respectful, soldiers nearest,
turn towards me, mark me well -
their duty always to listen,
mine, orders I have to sell.

This cannon never used in anger
does not rust, get out of date;
no grass dies or trees shake,
it doesn't matter if spring is late.

Horse-drawn wagons toil uphill,
trying to reach me endlessly;
nodding women sleep on baggage,
missing views of canal and sea.

Bringing up the never-ending rear,
proud men, stepping two by two -
scarlet and white, buttons shining,
muskets ready for nothing to do.

Down below, the barracks sparkle -
Georgian terrace - perpetually tall,
the landscaped fore-court evergreen,
not to be altered - buildings or wall.

Skittle soldiers on parade -
the 'Dismiss' order still to shout,
unendingly in stiff salute,
no one will ever bowl them out.

St. Leonard's church won't need repair,
the hill behind forever green -
no new houses to be built
or offices or things obscene.

The age of steam is about to begin
but this will never bother us,
together with Hythe, our barracks and sea
we will stay like this for eternity.

BLAME IT ON ETHELRED
(Villanelle)

Where winds still scream, sea and marsh mingle.
Ethelred levied tax on wine, a noisy affair,
the rattle of guns, tide hurling shingle.

His subjects thought the measure a swindle -
resorted to smuggling - those who would dare
where winds still scream, sea and marsh mingle.

Gangs met cutters cloaked in night, no jingle
of spur, with muffled hooves, they took great care,
the rattle of guns, tide hurling shingle.

Flogging Joey, Coastal Blockade - no single
measure could penetrate their secret lair,
where winds still scream, sea and marsh mingle.

In lonely churchyards, both sides commingle
King's men and smugglers deaf to the blare,
the rattle of guns, tide hurling shingle.

Parsons and poets whose fame won't dwindle
provoke Gentlemen's spirits - they plague the air
where winds still scream, sea and marsh mingle,
the rattle of guns, tide hurling shingle.

THE WEALD IN WINTER

Tightropewalkers, we tread the frozen
frames of yesterday's footprints,
glazed hollows of heel and toe
windows shattering in our wake.
Quickening the pace, sun flickers
a silent movie through slim trees
before they gang together, mouldering.

Snow now our only light;
this once impregnable forest
still casting shadows over four counties.
We shiver into scarves, gloves,
ducking to avoid icy branches
snagging our hair, spraying us with snow,
tipping our hats, making progress slow.

A clearing dead ahead;
sun spotlights a double elipsed pool,
ripples trapped seconds before their end -
a silver shield, bas-relief bordered,
stuck through by forest force
with huge sapling spears:
Andredsweald totem.

We take our fill, then slip away,
gatecrashers at a Private View.

DEBAUCHERY

   - of blossom vies with sky,
air craven with redolence:
apple, cherry, buds eased open,
wooed by impresario sun.

Cocked hats of oast house roundels
peer down on luminous snow -
prima donnas stole the show:
embarassed sheep avert their eyes,
pink white neons setting alight
Kent orchards in spring.

ICON

A spell of summer heat in February,
the magic promise of warmth.
Down hills rippled by ancient tides,
we walk towards the Rother, swollen golden,
marshes deluged after weeks of rain,
sun flashily reminding us of this gift
of the sea, and Oxney's salty cradle.

Backlit by fierce light, Rye fuses into one being;
the burnished city beckons: Avalon etched
on the horizon, its jagged outline climbing the hill
to the castellated tower, famed spire taut.
River like a glassy lake, holds the city captive:
antipodean twin turning hill into chasm,
cleft arm pointing to the lake's veiled depths.

A wooden barge rests at anchor, surrounded
by swans, mysterious otherworld queens; they glide
to the city more real than the original. It vanishes.
Our feet drawn where our hearts are loath to follow,
we cross the bridge, Quarter Boys chiming a salutation
from St. Mary's tower, our quest at an end.
For poet and painter the spell of fulfilment begins.

AMBASSADORS

I am brave Pocohontas, yearning for my home,
then Gladstone's General Gordon left in Khartoum, all alone,
the ghost of butchered Oldfield - Cooling Castle by the church,
and in Rochester, Miss Havisham, left in the lurch.

I am Coleridge home from Italy, leaping from a ship,
to give thanks at Lower Halstow, for the safety of my trip.
At Sittingbourne I hear ribald tales from Chaucer's pilgrims merry,
and the Arden scandal in Faversham, which they try so hard to bury.

It's cakes and ale at Whitstable, for I'm cynical Somerset Maugham,
I'm also Peter Cushing taking the horror movies by storm.
A Roman guard, I light a beacon, at high Reculver Fort,
Augustine at Ebbsfleet, I teach the religion I have brought.

Agricola, I sail from Sandwich, discover Britain is an isle,
and as Lady Hester Stanhope, at Walmer I raise a smile.
I am Lear at Shakespeare Cliff - a highly improbable drop,
whilst at Folkestone I circulate with Harvey's medical lot.

I am H.G. Wells at Sandgate in a house designed by Voysey,
and the basest of Becket's murderers, at Saltwood, that is me.
The Holy Maid of Kent, I perform miracles at Court-at-Street;
Erasmus, at Aldington, I find English more taxing than Greek.

Calling myself Ingoldsby, I write verse about times that are harsh,
and I face all manner of dangers, smuggling with Syn on the Marsh.
I coin, 'Live all you can', as Henry James, writing at Lamb House in Rye,
the end of the Saxon Shore Way walk, when I come back to being 'I'.